PRAYERSCRIPTS
Speaking God's Word Book Edition

DECLARE
Against
THE ENEMY

30 Days of Prayers for
SPEAKING GOD'S WORD BOLDLY TO ENFORCE TRIUMPH OVER DARKNESS

CYRIL OPOKU

Declare Against the Enemy: Speaking God's Word Boldly to Enforce Triumph Over Darkness

Published by *Quest Publications*

ISBN: 978-1-988439-80-8

Cover design by *Quest Publications (questpublications@outlook.com)*

Unless otherwise indicated, all Scripture quotations are taken from the World English Bible WEB, which is in the public domain. For more information, visit: www.worldenglish.bible

This book is a work of devotional encouragement. It is not intended to replace biblical study, pastoral counsel, or professional therapy.

Printed in the United States of America.

First Edition: August 2025

For more books like this, visit *PrayerScripts: https://prayerscripts.org*

CONTENTS

PREFACE

"Submit yourselves therefore to God. Resist the devil, and
he will flee from you."
—James 4:7 WEB

From the very first time I opened God's Word and prayed against the schemes of the enemy, I realized something profound: victory is not found in fear, strategies, or even in our own strength—it is found in aligning our voice and life with God's truth. This book, *Declare Against the Enemy*, was born from a personal journey of spiritual warfare, a journey marked by nights of prayer, moments of divine revelation, and the undeniable assurance that God's Word is sharper and more powerful than any force that rises against us.

I wrote this book for anyone who has ever felt the pressure of unseen battles or sensed that the enemy is working against their family, their destiny, or their peace. These pages are not filled with mere suggestions; they are prophetic declarations anchored in Scripture, designed to equip you to enforce God's victory in every area of your life. Each prayer is a deliberate, Spirit-led response to the tactics of darkness—crafted to empower your voice, embolden your faith, and awaken your authority in Christ.

As you journey through these prayers, know that you are not walking alone. I have stood in the same battles you face, and I have witnessed God's hand scatter every enemy scheme. My prayer is that you, too, will rise in confidence, courage, and authority, speaking life, triumph, and supernatural breakthrough over your life and the lives of those you love.

This is more than a book; it is a companion, a guide, and a weapon in your hands. May it stir your spirit, sharpen your voice, and release the power of God to destroy every plan of the enemy.

Ready at His command,
Cyril O. *(Illinois, August 2025)*

INTRODUCTION

Have you ever felt the invisible hands of the enemy pressing against your life, your family, or your destiny? Have you sensed the subtle, relentless attacks that seek to steal your peace, undermine your faith, or destroy your purpose? You are not alone. The spiritual realm is alive with forces that oppose the will of God, but Scripture reminds us that these forces are neither stronger nor wiser than the Almighty God who fights for us.

Declare Against the Enemy is a prophetic call to arms—a book designed to equip you to recognize, confront, and utterly defeat the schemes of darkness. Through these prayers, you will discover the power of speaking God's Word boldly, enforcing heaven's decrees, and seeing the spiritual strongholds of your life collapse under the authority of Christ. Each Scripture has been carefully chosen to reveal God's promises and to empower you to act decisively, turning fear into faith and oppression into triumph.

This book is a prophetic toolkit for believers who refuse to be passive in the face of evil. Here, every prayer is crafted to awaken your spiritual senses, sharpen your discernment, and arm you with the authority that Jesus Christ has already given you. You will not only pray—you will declare, enforce, and see victory manifest in your life.

As you journey through these pages, expect your spiritual eyes to open wider, your faith to rise higher, and your confidence in God's protection and provision to grow unshakeable. No longer will you be a silent observer of the enemy's schemes. Instead, you will rise as a bold warrior, equipped with Scripture, guided by the Spirit, and unstoppable in the authority of Jesus' name.

This is your moment to take your stand. The enemy will fight—but he will not prevail. God Himself has already gone before you, and through the Word, your voice becomes a weapon that enforces triumph over darkness.

Declare Against the Enemy. Your time to walk boldly in victory begins now.

How to Use This Book

This is not a book to be rushed through. Each of the 30 prayers is structured as a daily prayer journey, combining the Word of God with prophetic, Spirit-led intercession. Here's how you can make the most of it:

1. **Start with the Scripture** – Each prayer begins with a verse from the World English Bible (WEB). Read it slowly and aloud, letting the Word sink into your heart.

2. **Declare the Word** – Meditate on the key truth in the verse, affirming it as God's unchanging promise.

3. **Pray with Authority** – Use the written prayer as a guide. Speak it boldly, personally, and with conviction. Replace "I" with your name or the names of loved ones as needed.

4. **Journal Insights** – Keep a notebook nearby. Write down any impressions, warnings, or directions you sense from the Holy Spirit.

5. **Build a Rhythm** – Pray one Scripture each day, or linger longer on those that strike you deeply. Repetition builds sharpness, and sharpness builds victory.

Whether you walk through these prayers privately in your devotional time, with your family, or in a small group, the key is consistency. Each prayer is a sword in your hand—use it faithfully.

DAY 1

TRAMPLE EVERY SERPENT

"Behold, I give you authority to tread on serpents and
scorpions, and over all the power of the enemy. Nothing
will in any way hurt you."
— Luke 10:19 WEB

Mighty Warrior God, I rise today in the strength of Your promise,
declaring that I walk in the authority You have vested in me through
Christ Jesus. By Your word, I stand as one who is not a victim but a
victor, a soldier clothed in divine power to trample underfoot every
serpent and every scorpion that dares to approach my life or my
household.

I declare that the enemy's strategies are crushed beneath my feet.
Every demonic assignment, every whisper of fear, every chain of
affliction and oppression must bow, because the authority of Christ
reigns in me. I tread boldly, not by my own strength, but by the
living power of Your Spirit. Every serpent of deception, every
scorpion of destruction—your power is nullified, your poison
made void, your bite silenced forever.

Father, let the atmosphere around me and my family be charged
with Your power. I decree that no hidden trap, no secret ambush,
and no weapon formed in darkness can prevail against us. Angels
of the Lord, encamp around us as we enforce Christ's triumph over
all evil. I declare the enemy's grip is broken, his schemes exposed,
and his dominion destroyed.

With holy boldness, I walk unharmed through fire and storm, through valley and shadow, knowing that nothing by any means shall injure me or those covered under Your covenant. I enforce this victory over my family's health, our destiny, and our generations. What the enemy planned for harm is overturned and converted into testimonies of Your glory.

In Jesus' name, Amen.

DAY 2

Overcome by the Blood

"They overcame him because of the Lamb's blood, and
because of the word of their testimony. They didn't love
their life, even to death."
— Revelation 12:11 WEB

Lord of Hosts, I rise in the testimony of the Blood of the Lamb! By
that Blood, I declare the enemy is silenced, stripped of power, and
cast down in utter defeat. The blood of Jesus cries louder than the
accuser's voice, and I wield it as a weapon against every force that
contends with my soul and my family's destiny.

I decree that the blood secures my victory. Every accusation hurled
in the courts of heaven is overruled by the covenant of mercy sealed
at Calvary. My testimony is this: I am redeemed, I am cleansed, I
am untouchable, and I am more than a conqueror through Him
who loved me. No threat of darkness can overthrow what the blood
has already purchased.

O God, I lift my voice as a trumpet against the enemy. My words
align with heaven's decree, testifying that my household is covered,
our lineage is marked, and our inheritance is sealed. No plague, no
curse, no bondage, no tormenting spirit has legal ground here. The
blood is our banner and our fortress.

With holy defiance, I declare the adversary cast down. By the power
of testimony, I uproot lies, I scatter plots, and I demolish
strongholds. We overcome, we conquer, and we prevail—not by

might, not by power, but by the victory of the Cross and the eternal Blood of the Lamb.

In Jesus' name, Amen.

DAY 3

No Weapon Prevails

"No weapon that is formed against you will prevail; and you will condemn every tongue that rises against you in judgment. This is the heritage of Yahweh's servants, and their righteousness is of me," says Yahweh.
— Isaiah 54:17 WEB

Righteous Father, I take my stand in Your covenant promise: no weapon formed against me shall prevail. I rise as Your servant, clothed in righteousness that is not my own, but born of Your mercy and truth. Every weapon, seen and unseen, forged in secret or launched in open attack, is shattered by the fire of Your word.

I condemn every tongue that rises against me, against my family, against my calling. I silence accusations, lies, curses, and slanders spoken in the spirit realm or uttered by human lips. They carry no weight, no authority, no permanence, for my vindication comes from You, the Judge of all the earth.

Father, I declare that my household walks in the safety of this heritage. Arrows of sickness are broken, traps of poverty are dismantled, conspiracies of darkness are overturned. Every satanic design collapses into dust at the mention of the mighty name of Jesus.

I enforce Your covenant over my life: my future is secure, my path is ordered, my name is preserved in glory. The battle is not mine, but Yours, and the outcome is certain—victory, triumph, and dominion through the Lord Jesus Christ.

In Jesus' name, Amen.

DAY 4

MIGHTY WEAPONS OF GOD

"For the weapons of our warfare are not of the flesh, but mighty before God to the throwing down of strongholds, throwing down imaginations and every high thing that is exalted against the knowledge of God, and bringing every thought into captivity to the obedience of Christ."
— 2 Corinthians 10:4–5 WEB

Captain of Heaven's Armies, I rise in the power of Your divine arsenal. My weapons are not carnal, not of human design, but mighty in Your hands to demolish every fortress of darkness. I declare that no stronghold in my life or my family can withstand the fire of Your Spirit. Every chain is shattered, every prison is opened, every lie is exposed.

I cast down imaginations, deceitful philosophies, and mental fortresses raised against the truth of Christ. Every argument whispered by the enemy falls flat under the authority of Your word. I take captive every thought—every fear, every doubt, every whisper of defeat—and bind it to the obedience of Christ. Only Your truth reigns in my mind and my home.

Father, I decree that over my household, every high place erected against Your knowledge is torn down. Every altar of wickedness is dismantled, every spell is broken, every assignment overturned. My life is an altar of obedience, my mind is the dwelling of Christ's light, and my family is sealed under heaven's decree.

Let the fire of Your Spirit sweep through every corner of our being, consuming darkness, cleansing hearts, and establishing Your dominion. By these weapons, we do not just survive—we conquer, we reign, we triumph in the power of Christ's obedience.

In Jesus' name, Amen.

DAY 5

RESIST AND OVERCOME

"Be subject therefore to God. Resist the devil, and he will
flee from you."
— James 4:7 WEB

Holy and Sovereign Lord, I bow in full surrender to Your rule. My
strength is found in yielding to Your authority, and in this posture
of submission I rise with power to resist the adversary. My
allegiance is to You alone, and under the covering of Your throne,
no enemy can withstand the fire of resistance.

I declare that the devil is a defeated foe. His strategies crumble, his
lies dissolve, his presence is banished. By standing firmly in Your
word, I push back against his encroachment. Every place where he
seeks to gain ground in my life, my family, my health, and my
destiny—I resist with unyielding faith, and he flees seven ways.

Father, I enforce the truth that my family is not prey to the enemy's
schemes. His grip is broken, his claws torn away, his influence
destroyed. The banner of Your presence overshadows us, and Your
angels stand guard. Every door once open to darkness is sealed by
the blood of Jesus, and every chain is broken by the power of Your
Spirit.

I decree today: my household belongs to the Lord. No devil, no
spirit of oppression, no generational curse has authority here. We
are surrendered, we are secured, and we are shielded by the power

of Christ. The devil flees, but we remain, steadfast and victorious in Your covenant love.

In Jesus' name, Amen.

DAY 6

Strong in the Lord

"Finally, be strong in the Lord, and in the strength of his might. Put on the whole armor of God, that you may be able to stand against the wiles of the devil."
—Ephesians 6:10–11 WEB

Mighty Warrior and Captain of Heaven's Hosts, I rise today clothed in Your strength and girded with Your might. My frailty bows before Your everlasting power, and I declare that I am not weak, for the Lord is the strength of my life. By Your Spirit, I put on the full armor You have provided—Your truth, Your righteousness, the readiness of the gospel, the shield of faith, the helmet of salvation, and the sword of Your Word.

I decree that no scheme of the enemy will find me unprepared. I renounce every whisper of defeat, intimidation, and fear, for I am hidden in Christ and fortified by the armor of God. Every plan of darkness against my life, my family, and my destiny is thwarted by divine covering.

Father, I declare that I will not be a victim of the enemy's strategies. The weapons of deception, seduction, oppression, and confusion are shattered by Your truth and extinguished by faith's shield. By Your might, I stand upright and immovable, refusing to yield to any snare of the adversary.

Let Your strength flow like fire through my soul. As I march forward in Your armor, I trample upon every work of darkness. The wicked shall stumble and fall, for the Lord, my defender, equips me with power to prevail. I stand, unshaken, victorious in Christ.

In Jesus' name, Amen.

DAY 7

ARMED FOR BATTLE

"For our wrestling is not against flesh and blood, but
against the principalities, against the powers, against the
world's rulers of the darkness of this age, and against the
spiritual forces of wickedness in the heavenly places.
Therefore put on the whole armor of God, that you may
be able to withstand in the evil day, and having done all, to
stand."
—Ephesians 6:12–13 WEB

Eternal King, I rise with clarity of spirit, discerning that my battle
is not with men but with invisible forces arrayed in wickedness. I
refuse to be distracted by human opposition, for I see beyond the
natural into the realm of the spirit where the true enemies dwell.
Today I take my stand, fully clothed in the armor of God, declaring
that I will not be moved.

Lord of Hosts, I confront every principality and power aligned
against me. I decree that their altars are overturned, their decrees
are annulled, and their assignments are cast down. By the blood of
the Lamb and the word of my testimony, I nullify every demonic
resistance raised against my destiny and my family.

Father, in this evil day, I am girded with Your truth, my heart is
guarded by righteousness, and my faith extinguishes the arrows of
hell. I take up the sword of Your Word to pierce through every
darkness, declaring that no enemy will have dominion over me.

I stand immovable, declaring that my house belongs to the Lord, my body is a temple of the Holy Spirit, and my path is marked by victory. Every demonic wrestling match ends in defeat, for the Lord has given me power to overcome.

In Jesus' name, Amen.

DAY 8

Dwelling in God's Shadow

"He who dwells in the secret place of the Most High will
rest in the shadow of the Almighty. I will say of Yahweh,
'He is my refuge and my fortress; my God, in whom I
trust.'"
—Psalm 91:1–2 WEB

Most High God, I run into Your secret place and choose to abide
under the shadow of Your wings. There, no darkness can penetrate,
no arrow can strike, and no enemy can prevail. You are my eternal
dwelling, my hiding place, my fortress, and my covering shield.

I declare with my mouth and believe in my heart: You alone are my
God, my strong tower, my unshakable refuge. The schemes of the
enemy cannot infiltrate the sanctuary of Your presence. My family
is hidden under Your shadow, where no harm can reach us.

Father, as I rest in Your Almighty shadow, I decree that fear will not
govern me. The snares of the wicked are broken, and the lies of the
adversary are silenced. I will not live in anxiety, for my trust is fixed
on the Rock of Ages.

I speak forth that my dwelling is not exposed to the storms of hell,
but established in the fortress of God. Every spirit of violence, every
demonic storm, every satanic decree passes over me, for I am
shielded by the Lord of Glory.

In Jesus' name, Amen.

DAY 9

ANGELS ON ASSIGNMENT

"No evil shall happen to you, neither shall any plague come near your dwelling. For he will put his angels in charge of you, to guard you in all your ways."
—Psalm 91:10–11 WEB

Faithful Father, I declare that no evil will overtake me, no calamity will enter my house, and no plague will defile my dwelling. Your covenant word stands over me as an unbreakable shield, and I claim it for myself and my household.

By Your decree, angels are stationed around my life. I release them now in the name of Jesus to guard me in every pathway I tread. Their fiery presence drives back every demonic intruder, uproots every satanic trap, and secures my journey in peace.

Lord of Hosts, I stand in boldness declaring that sickness, destruction, and evil visitation shall not be my portion. Every curse spoken against me is overturned by angelic enforcement. My family is surrounded by the armies of heaven, and no hand of the wicked can touch us.

I proclaim divine safety in my dwelling. I proclaim supernatural protection in my going out and my coming in. Every hidden plot of the adversary collapses before the angels on assignment, and every evil spirit retreats in terror.

In Jesus' name, Amen.

DAY 10

Scattered Before My Face

"Yahweh will cause your enemies who rise up against you
to be struck before you. They will come out against you
one way, and will flee before you seven ways."
—Deuteronomy 28:7 WEB

Lord of Hosts, my Banner and Deliverer, I rise in victory today declaring that every enemy rising against me is struck down by Your mighty hand. Their weapons are shattered, their plans frustrated, and their gatherings scattered to nothingness.

I decree that those who advance against my life and family come in one way, but by Your power, they scatter in seven. Confusion is their portion, defeat is their inheritance, and disgrace is their end. None can prevail against the anointed of the Lord.

Father, I thank You for fighting for me. The battles waged in secret against my destiny are overturned, and the arrows shot in darkness return upon the heads of the wicked. My path is secured by Your covenant promise, and my house is guarded by Your faithfulness.

I proclaim that no spiritual pursuer, no demonic attacker, no satanic adversary shall stand before me. They fall by the sword of the Spirit, and they flee by the terror of the Lord. I walk in triumph, for You have declared me victorious.

In Jesus' name, Amen.

DAY 11

More Than a Conqueror

"But in all these things, we are more than conquerors through him who loved us."
—Romans 8:37 WEB

Mighty God, Captain of my salvation, I rise in the confidence of Your unshakable Word. You have decreed that in every battle, trial, and opposition, I am not merely a survivor, but more than a conqueror through Christ who loves me. Today, I declare that no enemy scheme, no demonic assault, and no wicked voice will prevail over my life or my family, for Your love has already sealed our victory.

I boldly enforce this heavenly verdict upon the earth. I decree that every force of darkness aligned against my destiny is overthrown. The enemy may attempt to afflict, but I am not defeated. I am seated with Christ in victory, clothed with His triumph, and walking in His authority. My household is wrapped in this covering of divine conquest, and every attack crumbles under the weight of His love and power.

Father, I declare that discouragement, fear, sickness, and oppression cannot dominate us. Your love has secured our triumph, and I wield that truth like a sword against every lying voice. My confession is that the blood of Jesus has sealed our victory, and no power of hell can reverse it.

By this declaration, I establish a hedge of victory around my family. No curse, spell, or demonic assignment will prosper. We march forward in conquest, not by our strength, but through Christ who loves us beyond measure.

In Jesus' name, Amen.

DAY 12

SPOILING THE PRINCIPALITIES

"Having stripped the principalities and the powers, he made a show of them openly, triumphing over them in it."
—Colossians 2:15 WEB

King of Glory, I lift my voice to exalt the One who triumphed on the cross. Jesus, by Your sacrifice, You disarmed principalities and powers, paraded them in defeat, and declared eternal victory. Today, I enforce that triumph over every work of darkness that dares to challenge my destiny.

I declare that every demonic stronghold erected against me is already dismantled. Every ancient chain is broken because my Lord stripped the enemy of his weapons. No curse, no enchantment, and no hidden attack can succeed, for You, Jesus, have spoiled their arsenal and publicly displayed their powerlessness. I stand in this victory, and I enforce it over my life and my family.

By the authority of the risen Christ, I proclaim that every satanic conspiracy is overturned. Where the enemy seeks to steal peace, I declare restoration. Where he attempts to sow confusion, I declare divine clarity. Where he launches arrows of sickness or fear, I declare healing and boldness. The triumph of Calvary resounds in my home, my lineage, and my future.

O Lord of Hosts, I rejoice that the cross has silenced every accuser. I enforce this victory in the heavens and on earth, declaring that no devil will reclaim what Christ has stripped away. My family walks in freedom because the enemy has already been spoiled.

In Jesus' name, Amen.

DAY 13

GREATER WITHIN ME

"You are of God, little children, and have overcome them; because greater is he who is in you than he who is in the world."
—1 John 4:4 WEB

Sovereign Lord, I lift my voice in triumph, for I am born of You, and I have already overcome. The Greater One dwells within me, towering above every force arrayed against my destiny. I declare that no power of the world, no scheme of darkness, and no voice of the adversary can overthrow the One who lives in me.

I speak forth this truth over my household: the Spirit of the Living God within us is superior to every attack, stronger than every curse, and mightier than every adversary. I decree that demonic forces operating against our peace, our health, or our progress are subdued. They cannot contend with the One enthroned in our hearts.

I declare that the Greater One in me manifests in wisdom, in power, and in discernment. Every deception of the enemy is unmasked. Every weapon he forms shatters before it strikes. The world and its rulers may roar, but they collapse under the weight of the presence of the Almighty within me.

Father, I enforce this greater reality. My children, my family, and all connected to me walk under the covering of the Greater One.

Darkness cannot invade, for the light of God shines brighter and overcomes. This victory is eternal, irreversible, and unstoppable.

In Jesus' name, Amen.

DAY 14

DESTROYING THE THIEF'S AGENDA

"The thief only comes to steal, kill, and destroy. I came that
they may have life, and may have it abundantly."
—John 10:10 WEB

Living Christ, Shepherd of my soul, I exalt You for coming to give
me abundant life. By Your authority, I stand to declare that the thief
and all his destructive plans are nullified. I renounce every satanic
agenda designed to rob, to slay, and to devastate my life and my
family.

I decree that the enemy will not steal my joy, my peace, or my
destiny. Every demonic hand stretched toward my household is
withered. Every scheme of destruction collapses into nothing. My
family will not be devoured, for You, Lord Jesus, have granted us
overflowing life that cannot be quenched by the enemy.

I boldly declare that we live in the abundance of Your Spirit. Where
the adversary attempts to sow death, I enforce resurrection life.
Where he seeks to scatter, I declare divine order and restoration.
Where he sends poverty, I decree abundance. Where he releases
fear, I declare bold faith. The thief's mission is canceled, and Christ's
mission prevails.

Father, I embrace the abundance You promised, and I enforce it
upon every area of my life. My marriage, my children, my ministry,
and my work are saturated with Your overflowing life. No demonic

power has the authority to drain or destroy what You have ordained for me.

In Jesus' name, Amen.

DAY 15

THE KEYS OF AUTHORITY

"I also tell you that you are Peter, and on this rock I will build my assembly, and the gates of Hades will not prevail against it. I will give to you the keys of the Kingdom of Heaven, and whatever you bind on earth will have been bound in heaven; and whatever you release on earth will have been released in heaven."
—Matthew 16:18–19 WEB

Lord Jesus, Builder of Your Church and Keeper of the keys, I lift up my voice to declare Your unshakable promise. You have established Your assembly on the Rock, and no gate of Hades can withstand it. I declare that my life, my family, and my destiny are aligned with this victorious foundation.

I stand in the authority of the Kingdom, wielding the keys You have entrusted. I bind every force of darkness that rises against me. I bind spirits of infirmity, confusion, and oppression. I bind ancestral curses and demonic patterns seeking to repeat destruction in my family line. In their place, I loose the blessings of heaven—peace, healing, restoration, and favor.

I declare that every evil gate erected against my household collapses now. The gates of sickness, the gates of poverty, the gates of delay, and the gates of premature death cannot prevail. By divine authority, I shut doors the enemy has opened and I open doors of grace, breakthrough, and abundant life.

Mighty God, I decree that my family and I walk in victory. The authority of heaven backs every word I release. The adversary cannot overturn it, for the Rock of Christ stands eternal, and the Church You are building will never fall.

In Jesus' name, Amen.

DAY 16

STAND FIRM AND SEE

> Moses said to the people, "Don't be afraid. Stand still, and see the salvation of Yahweh, which he will work for you today; for the Egyptians whom you have seen today, you shall never see them again. Yahweh will fight for you, and you shall be still."
> —Exodus 14:13–14 WEB

O Lord of Hosts, the Mighty Man of War, I rise today in Your unfailing strength. You are my Deliverer who parts the seas before me and silences the armies behind me. I lift my voice in bold declaration that I will not fear, for You are fighting on my behalf. Every enemy that has risen against my life, my household, my destiny, shall fall and never rise again.

I declare in faith that the strongholds of oppression and torment are broken by the arm of the Lord. The chariots of darkness pursuing me are swallowed up by the waters of Your power. My family and I shall cross into promise-land territory, untouched and unharmed, while the wicked are drowned in their own schemes.

Father, I align myself with Your Word and command peace into my soul. I will be still, not because of weakness, but because of confidence in Your strength. I will not strive in human flesh, but I will rest in the assurance that You are my salvation.

Let the voice of fear be silenced. Let the spirit of intimidation crumble. Let the enemy's pursuit end in his own destruction. I boldly declare that every attack against my life is reversed and every weapon forged against me is shattered. I see the salvation of the Lord today and forever.

In Jesus' name, Amen.

DAY 17

FEAR NOT, I AM WITH YOU

"Don't you be afraid, for I am with you. Don't be dismayed, for I am your God. I will strengthen you. Yes, I will help you. Yes, I will uphold you with the right hand of my righteousness."
—Isaiah 41:10 WEB

Everlasting Father, I lift my voice in confidence today, declaring that I will not fear, for You are with me. Your righteous right hand upholds me and my family, securing us against every scheme of the wicked one. You are my God, unshaken and unchanging, and I rest in the fortress of Your strength.

I decree that no demonic intimidation shall stand before me. The enemy's whispers of despair, anxiety, and hopelessness are cast down in the name of Jesus. I receive divine courage, for the Almighty has chosen me and surrounded me with His everlasting arms. Where weakness has tried to overtake me, I proclaim supernatural strength; where discouragement has pressed upon me, I announce heavenly help.

Lord, I exalt You as my Shield and Sustainer. Uphold me in righteousness, and let my enemies stumble in confusion. May every satanic agenda assigned to my family be scattered, and every yoke of oppression be broken. I stand under the covering of Your power, unshaken and victorious.

Today I boldly declare that I am upheld, strengthened, and kept by the Lord who never abandons His own. Fear is banished, despair is overturned, and courage rises in my spirit. I shall walk in triumph, for You are with me.

In Jesus' name, Amen.

DAY 18

REJOICE OVER THE FALL

"Don't rejoice against me, my enemy. When I fall, I will
arise. When I sit in darkness, Yahweh will be a light to me."
—Micah 7:8 WEB

Almighty God, my Refuge and Light, I rise to declare that the
enemy will not triumph over me. Though I have stumbled, I will
arise. Though darkness has tried to overshadow me, Your radiant
light shines brighter and pierces the gloom. My enemies shall not
rejoice at my downfall, for You lift me up in glory.

I decree that every satanic laughter over my setbacks is silenced.
Every plot that sought to bury me shall become the platform of my
rising. My family will not be defeated; instead, we will stand as
witnesses of the resurrection power of Christ Jesus. When despair
tried to chain me, Your light shattered its hold. When shame tried
to cover me, Your hand lifted me into honor.

Lord, let every dark valley become a highway of victory. Let every
shadow be dispelled by the brightness of Your presence. I speak
against cycles of oppression, depression, and confusion

—they are broken by the light of the Lord.

Today, I boldly proclaim that I am not defined by my fall but by my
rising. I am not caged by darkness but carried by light. The enemy
will not mock me, for the Lord has already decreed my restoration.

In Jesus' name, Amen.

DAY 19

THE LORD MY LIGHT

Yahweh is my light and my salvation. Whom shall I fear?
Yahweh is the strength of my life. Of whom shall I be
afraid? When evildoers came at me to eat up my flesh,
even my adversaries and my foes, they stumbled and fell.
—Psalm 27:1–2 WEB

Mighty Deliverer, I lift my voice in faith to proclaim that You are
my light, my salvation, and my strength. No darkness can withstand
Your glory, and no enemy can consume me, for You surround me
with Your power. Fear has no claim on my life, for the Lord of Hosts
is my Defender.

I decree that every adversary that rises against me and my
household shall stumble and fall. Those who seek to devour my
flesh, my health, my peace, and my destiny shall collapse under the
weight of Your judgment. You are my Shield and Fortress, and in
You I am secure.

Lord, I reject the spirit of fear and declare boldness in Your name.
The arrows of the wicked shall not strike me, and the snares of
darkness shall not entangle my feet. Your strength is my portion,
and Your salvation is my song.

Today, I stand under the banner of victory, declaring that the light
of Christ shines over every hidden work of darkness. Let the power
of my enemies be dismantled and their weapons destroyed. I rejoice
in Your salvation, for You have secured my triumph.

In Jesus' name, Amen.

DAY 20

DELIVERED FROM THE STRONG ENEMY

He delivered me from my strong enemy, from those who
hated me; for they were too mighty for me.
—Psalm 18:17 WEB

O Lord, my Rock and my Redeemer, I declare that You have
delivered me from the grip of the mighty foe. Though the enemy
was stronger than I, he was no match for the power of my God. The
oppressors who hated me, who rose against my destiny, have been
cast down by Your mighty hand.

I decree that every strong enemy contending with my family and
me is broken by the authority of Jesus' blood. The chains of hatred,
curses, and generational afflictions are shattered. No stronghold of
darkness can prevail against the strong arm of the Lord. You are my
Deliverer, and I walk in freedom purchased by Christ.

Father, I exalt You as the One who rescues and sustains. Though the
enemy sought to overwhelm me, You have lifted me above his
reach. Though he was too mighty for me, he could not withstand
the might of my God. My household is untouchable, secured under
the covering of divine deliverance.

I boldly proclaim that victory is mine. The strong enemy is
defeated, his grip broken, his schemes nullified. I stand free, my
head lifted in triumph, because the Lord has delivered me.

In Jesus' name, Amen.

DAY 21

Many Are the Afflictions

"Many are the afflictions of the righteous, but Yahweh delivers him out of them all."
—Psalm 34:19 WEB

Mighty Deliverer, my refuge and my strength, I lift my voice with boldness to declare that every affliction assigned against me and my household is shattered under the weight of Your covenant faithfulness. Though battles rage, though storms rise, though arrows fly in the day and terrors lurk in the night, I declare that none shall overcome me, for You, O Lord, are the Deliverer of the righteous.

I declare that every chain the enemy has wrapped around my family is broken. Every sickness, setback, oppression, and cycle of hardship bows to the power of the Deliverer. My household shall not be consumed by trouble, for the Word of the Lord has gone forth: You deliver us from them all. Father, I enforce that victory over my home, over my children, over my destiny, and over every assignment of darkness.

Let the voice of affliction be silenced now. Let the tormentor be overthrown. Every stronghold of fear, pain, and despair must collapse under the thunder of Your power. What the enemy meant for my destruction, Lord, You turn for my triumph. You have set my feet in a large place, far from the snare of the fowler and far from the pit of destruction.

I boldly declare that my family and I are untouchable under Your delivering hand. We shall walk through fire and not be burned; through deep waters and not be drowned. Trouble will not dictate our destiny. Afflictions will not define our story. Your Word has spoken, and I declare it: deliverance is ours today and always.

In Jesus' name, Amen.

DAY 22

THE LORD IS FAITHFUL

"But the Lord is faithful, who will establish you, and guard
you from the evil one."
—2 Thessalonians 3:3 WEB

Faithful God, covenant-keeping King, I stand today declaring that
Your faithfulness is my fortress. No power of darkness, no strategy
of the enemy, no deception of hell can undo the shield You have set
around me. You are the God who establishes me, and I declare that
every shaking in my life is silenced under the firmness of Your
Word.

I decree that my family is guarded by the Almighty. Every attack of
the evil one—whether by disease, confusion, temptation, or fear—
dies before it reaches our gates. I declare angelic covering over my
dwelling, supernatural preservation over my mind, and unshakable
stability in my walk with You. O Lord, establish me in Your truth
and root me in Your Word, that no wind of doctrine, no storm of
adversity, and no fiery dart may uproot me.

Where the enemy seeks to destabilize, You strengthen. Where the
adversary plots ambush, You guard. I declare today that my destiny
is sealed by divine faithfulness, not the fickle schemes of men or
devils. Let the roaring of the wicked be silenced. Let every snare be
exposed and destroyed. The evil one has no foothold, no power, no
claim over my life or my household.

Father, I declare stability. I declare protection. I declare that You, the Faithful One, guard me day and night. My life is not left vulnerable to the adversary's plans, for You are the Keeper of Israel who never slumbers. I rise in boldness to enforce this truth—my family is shielded, my destiny is preserved, my future is secured.

In Jesus' name, Amen.

DAY 23

Stand Firm in Faith

"Be sober and self-controlled. Be watchful. Your adversary, the devil, walks around like a roaring lion, seeking whom he may devour. Withstand him steadfast in your faith, knowing that your brothers who are in the world are undergoing the same sufferings."
—1 Peter 5:8–9 WEB

Lord of Hosts, my Banner in battle, I declare that the roar of the adversary will not intimidate me nor devour my family. Though he prowls and seeks to steal, kill, and destroy, I rise as a warrior of faith, standing firm in the victory of the cross. I will not be shaken. I will not be deceived. My eyes are open, my spirit alert, my heart guarded by the Word.

I decree that every deceptive roar of the enemy falls silent. Every intimidation, fear, and anxiety designed to paralyze me is overthrown. I resist the devil today, not in my strength but in the steadfast faith You have given me. His plots are exposed, his strategies dismantled, and his snares destroyed by the authority of Jesus Christ.

My family will not be prey for the roaring lion. My children will not be devoured. My household will not be consumed by hidden snares. I enforce the power of resistance through the blood of the Lamb, declaring that we are untouchable, steadfast, and immovable in our faith.

As I stand, Lord, I stand not alone but with a company of believers across the world. Together, we are a mighty army, rising with unshakable faith, overcoming the roaring lies with the roar of the Lion of Judah. The adversary is resisted, and the victory is enforced. In Jesus' name, Amen.

DAY 24

AFFLICTION WILL NOT RISE AGAIN

"What do you plot against Yahweh? He will make a full end. Affliction won't rise up the second time."
—Nahum 1:9 WEB

Sovereign Judge, consuming Fire, I lift my voice in holy defiance against every scheme plotted against me and my family. The enemy's designs are overturned, for no power can stand against You. I declare that the plots of darkness against my household are nullified. Every demonic agenda, every curse, every hidden plan is consumed by the fire of the Almighty.

I enforce the decree of heaven: affliction shall not rise a second time. The pain of yesterday will not repeat. The bondage of former days will not return. Cycles of failure, cycles of sickness, cycles of oppression, cycles of delay—by the authority of Your Word, they are broken forever. My life is not a playground for recurring battles. My family is not a dwelling for repeated afflictions.

O Lord, make a full end of the works of darkness. Render them powerless, empty, and void. Let the enemy's camp be scattered, and his schemes brought to nothing. The battles that once consumed us will not return, for the hand of the Almighty has declared the end from the beginning.

I rise boldly in faith and announce that the blood of Jesus speaks permanence over our deliverance. No generational affliction, no repeated attack, no familiar spirit shall revisit us. We stand sealed by the covenant, established in victory, and shielded by divine authority.

In Jesus' name, Amen.

DAY 25

THE CAPTIVES SHALL BE DELIVERED

"But Yahweh says, 'Even the captives of the mighty shall be taken away, and the prey of the terrible shall be delivered; for I will contend with him who contends with you, and I will save your children.'"
—Isaiah 49:25 WEB

Mighty Redeemer, Captain of my salvation, I rise to declare Your Word with authority and fire. You are the One who breaks chains and plunders the strongman's house. Today I decree that every captivity in my life and in my household is broken. Every prison of the enemy, every cage of affliction, every trap of oppression is shattered by the voice of the Lord.

I declare that the prey of the terrible is delivered. No matter how fierce the adversary, Your power is greater. My family will not remain in the grip of the oppressor. My children will not be swallowed by darkness. My destiny will not be held hostage. The Lord Himself contends with every contender, fights every battle, and overturns every adversary.

O Lord, rise as a Mighty Warrior and fight for me. Let the captives be released. Let the cords be cut. Let the prey be delivered. By Your hand, the captor is overthrown, and the oppressed are set free. The mighty and terrible shall bow to the Lord of Hosts.

I boldly declare salvation over my household. I enforce freedom over my lineage. I decree that my children are saved, preserved, and secured in You. Every claim of the enemy over their lives is revoked. Every chain binding their destiny is broken. Lord, You contend for us, and therefore we walk in victory.

In Jesus' name, Amen.

DAY 26

Unshaken by the Battle

"They will fight against you, but they will not prevail against you; for I am with you," says Yahweh, "to rescue you."
—Jeremiah 1:19 WEB

O Mighty Deliverer, today I rise in holy defiance against the enemies of my soul. Though battles rage and forces of darkness seek to overthrow me, Your Word declares that they will not prevail. I take my stand in this unshakable truth: You are with me to rescue and deliver. No power, no scheme, no plot of hell shall succeed against me or my household.

Lord of Hosts, I boldly declare that every rising adversary falls in defeat before Your presence in my life. The counsel of the wicked is confounded, and the hands lifted in war against me are broken. You are my shield and fortress, and because You stand beside me, no weapon formed against me can prosper. Every attack launched in the night is shattered by the light of Your presence.

Father, I enforce my triumph through Your Word. My family is preserved under Your mighty hand, and every demonic plot against our destiny is overturned. I speak life where the enemy has spoken death, peace where he has stirred confusion, and joy where he has attempted sorrow.

I decree that we rise victorious, rescued by Your hand, untouchable in the covenant of Your promises. Let the enemy be scattered in seven directions, while I remain steadfast, upheld by Your unfailing arm.

In Jesus' name, Amen.

DAY 27

THE MOUNTAIN MUST MOVE

Then he answered and spoke to me, saying, "This is
Yahweh's word to Zerubbabel, saying, 'Not by might, nor
by power, but by my Spirit,' says Yahweh of Armies. Who
are you, great mountain? Before Zerubbabel, you are a
plain; and he will bring out the capstone with shouts of
'Grace, grace, to it!'"
—Zechariah 4:6–7 WEB

Sovereign Lord, I lift my voice in triumph, for my victory is not
rooted in human strength but in the power of Your Spirit. By divine
decree, I confront every mountain of opposition that has risen
against me and my family. You, the Lord of Armies, declare that
such obstacles shall melt into nothing before Your Spirit's breath.

Today I proclaim that mountains of generational bondage are
leveled. Strongholds of darkness crumble, and the walls of
resistance are turned into plains. What the enemy has set before me
as immovable barriers dissolve by the authority of Your Spirit
within me. I shout grace, grace over every assignment of the
wicked, over every plot against my destiny, and over every
hindrance raised against my household.

Father, I declare that my path is made straight, my progress
unhindered, my breakthrough undeniable. By Your Spirit, I am
empowered to finish every divine assignment with strength, joy,

and glory. The hand of the enemy is broken, and the mountains of despair, delay, and defeat are reduced to nothingness before me.

I decree that my life testifies of Your Spirit's power, and my household stands as a monument of Your grace. What seemed impossible is made possible by You, O Lord.

In Jesus' name, Amen.

DAY 28

THE DESTROYER DEFEATED

Since then the children have shared in flesh and blood, he also himself in the same way partook of the same, that through death he might bring to nothing him who had the power of death, that is, the devil.
—Hebrews 2:14 WEB

O Conquering King, I lift my voice in victory, declaring that the devil, the accuser, the destroyer, has been rendered powerless through the death of Jesus Christ. No longer does death reign over me or my family, for Christ, the Eternal Victor, has crushed the one who held that power. I stand boldly in the triumph of the cross, declaring that the blood of Jesus has silenced the voice of death forever.

Father, I decree that every shadow of fear is dispelled. The enemy's threats against my life, my health, and my family's future are brought to nothing. He who once sought to enslave us through terror is now chained, defeated, and humiliated at the foot of the cross. I declare that we live, move, and breathe under the banner of life eternal, secured in Christ's sacrifice.

O God of glory, by Your Son's death and resurrection, I proclaim freedom over every chain of bondage. My family walks in the light of liberty, untouched by the grip of death, immune to the curse of destruction. The dominion of darkness has been shattered, and the resurrection life of Christ flows through us like a river of triumph.

I declare boldly: the devil is nothing, Christ is everything, and we are forever victorious.

In Jesus' name, Amen.

DAY 29

FIGHT THE GOOD FIGHT

Fight the good fight of faith. Take hold of the eternal life
to which you were called, and you confessed the good
confession in the sight of many witnesses.
—1 Timothy 6:12 WEB

Captain of my salvation, I rise today with sword in hand and shield lifted high, ready to fight the good fight of faith. I do not shrink back, nor do I cower before the enemy's roar. I take hold of the eternal life given to me, and I confess boldly before heaven and earth that Jesus Christ is Lord over me and my household.

Father, I declare that the fight has already been won by the blood of Christ, and I enforce that victory in every area of my life. I resist the enemy's lies with the truth of Your Word. I push back against the forces of darkness with the light of Christ burning within me. I refuse to surrender ground, for You have called me to stand, to contend, and to prevail.

By faith, I seize every promise You have spoken. I secure healing for my body, peace for my mind, provision for my family, and destiny for my children. No power of hell can strip from me the inheritance You have sealed in Christ Jesus. My confession is steadfast, my heart unwavering, my spirit aflame with holy courage.

I decree that my life is a living testimony of victorious faith. The enemy's grip is broken, and I march forward, clothed in the full armor of God, triumphant in every battle.

In Jesus' name, Amen.

DAY 30

HEAVEN'S COURTROOM AUTHORITY

"Most certainly I tell you, whatever things you bind on earth will have been bound in heaven, and whatever things you release on earth will have been released in heaven."
—Matthew 18:18 WEB

Righteous Judge of heaven and earth, I rise in the authority of Your Word to decree and enforce heaven's verdict over my life and family. Today I stand in the courtroom of heaven, armed with divine authority to bind and loose according to Your will. I declare that what heaven has bound shall be bound in me, and what heaven has loosed shall flow freely into my household.

I bind every work of darkness that seeks to steal, kill, or destroy. I chain the spirits of fear, sickness, confusion, and poverty, declaring their power nullified in my life. I forbid their operation, for heaven itself has decreed their defeat through the cross of Christ. By the authority vested in me through the blood, I decree that they have no entry, no voice, and no influence in my household.

I loose the blessings of heaven over my family. I release peace, joy, and divine health. I release favor, provision, and supernatural breakthroughs. I decree open heavens over my home, angelic protection over my children, and prosperity over our work. What has been loosed in heaven is loosed now on earth in me.

Father, I enforce heaven's agenda against the enemy's schemes. My words align with Yours, and my decrees echo the authority of Christ. What I declare stands, for heaven backs me with divine power.

In Jesus' name, Amen.

EPILOGUE

Standing Unshakable in Authority

As you reach the end of *Declare Against the Enemy*, know that this is not the conclusion of your journey—it is only the beginning. The prayers you have prayed, the Scriptures you have spoken, and the authority you have embraced are seeds planted in the soil of your life. Like every seed, they must be nurtured, protected, and activated daily. Spiritual victory is not a one-time event; it is a lifestyle of declaring God's Word, resisting the enemy, and walking boldly in the authority Christ has given you.

The enemy will continue to test, challenge, and provoke, but now you have a weapon in your mouth and a shield in your heart. I challenge you to maintain this posture of spiritual vigilance. Speak boldly over every area of your life and your family's life. Bind what should be bound, loose what should be loosed, and enforce the promises of heaven with unwavering faith. Let every day be a declaration that the forces of darkness have no place in your destiny.

Remember, the power of God is not limited by circumstance, fear, or opposition. Your voice, guided by Scripture, carries the same authority that Jesus Himself entrusted to His followers. Keep rising, keep declaring, and keep walking in victory, even when the battles feel relentless.

Your challenge is clear: do not allow complacency to steal the triumph you have been given. Stand unshakable. Declare unceasingly. And watch as heaven continues to fight for you, making every enemy scatter at the sound of your prophetic voice.

The war is ongoing, but your victory is certain. The authority is yours—use it boldly, consistently, and without hesitation.

In Jesus' name, Amen.

ENCOURAGE OTHERS WITH YOUR STORY

If this prayer guide has strengthened your faith, deepened your intercession, or helped you stand in the gap, would you consider leaving a short review on Amazon? Your feedback not only encourages others but also helps more believers discover this resource and join in the prayer movement. Every review—just a few sentences—makes a difference. Thank you for being part of this movement.

MORE FROM PRAYERSCRIPTS

COMMAND YOUR DESTINY SERIES

Command Your Morning:

30 Days of Prayers and Declarations to Seize Your Day and Shape Your Destiny

There is a battle over every morning—and every believer must choose to either drift into the day or command it.

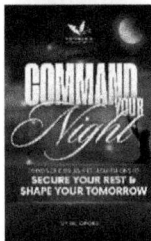

Command Your Night:

30 Days of Prayers and Declarations to Secure Your Rest and Shape Your Tomorrow

Every night is a spiritual battlefield—what you do before you sleep can determine the course of your tomorrow.

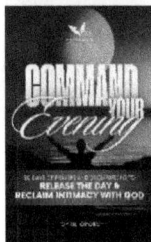

Command Your Evening:

30 Days of Prayers and Declarations to Release the Day and Reclaim Intimacy with God

There is a battle over every transition—and evening is one of the most spiritually neglected.

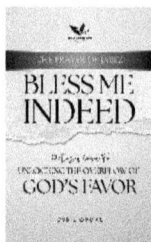

Bless Me Indeed:

Unlocking the Overflow of God's Favor

What if you could activate God's favor in your life today and walk in blessings that surpass your wildest expectations?

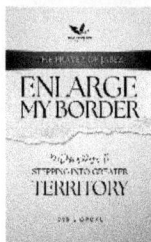

Enlarge My Border:

Stepping Into Greater Territory

Do you feel like you're living beneath your full potential? Do limitations, setbacks, and invisible barriers keep you from stepping into all God has promised? It's time to lift your cry for enlargement.

May Your Hand Be With Me:

Living Under Divine Power and Presence

What happens when the mighty hand of God rests upon your life? Doors open that no man can shut. Strength rises where weakness once prevailed. Guidance comes in the midst of confusion, and protection surrounds you in every battle.

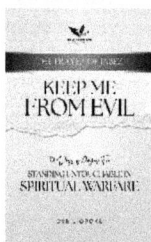

Keep Me From Evil:

Standing Untouchable in Spiritual Warfare

What if the enemy's plans could never touch you or your family? Imagine walking through life completely protected, untouchable, and victorious—no matter what schemes are formed against you.

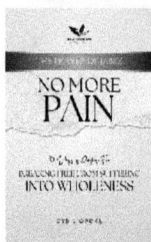

No More Pain:

Breaking Free from Suffering into Wholeness

Have you been carrying the weight of sorrow, disappointment, or hidden wounds for far too long? Do cycles of pain seem to repeat in your life, your marriage, or your family?

Discern the Enemy:

Sharpening Spiritual Perception to Recognize Satan's Tactics and Guard Your Destiny

The greatest danger is not the enemy you can see—it is the one you cannot. Can you recognize the enemy before he strikes?

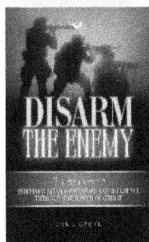

Disarm the Enemy:

Stripping Satan of Weapons and Influence Through the Power of Christ

Are you tired of feeling like the enemy has the upper hand in your life? It's time to take back your ground, silence the lies of darkness, and walk in the unstoppable authority of Christ.

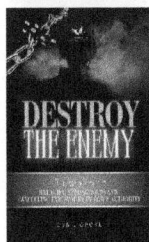

Destroy the Enemy:

Breaking Strongholds and Cancelling Evil Works by God's Authority

Are you tired of living under the weight of unseen battles? It's time to rise up and destroy the enemy's works in your life.

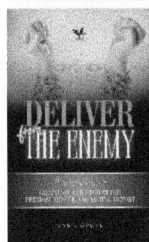

Deliver from the Enemy:

Calling on God's Power for Freedom, Rescue, and Lasting Victory

Break free from spiritual attacks and experience God's mighty deliverance in every battle.

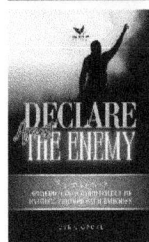

Declare Against the Enemy:

Speaking God's Word Boldly to Enforce Triumph Over Darkness

What if you could silence the enemy's schemes, protect your family, and walk boldly into every God-ordained assignment with unshakable authority?

Scriptures & Prayers for Deliverance from Trouble:

40 Days of Prayer for When Life Feels Overwhelming

Are you walking through a season where life feels heavy and your prayers feel weak?

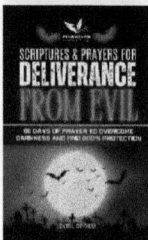

Scriptures & Prayers for Deliverance from Evil:

50 Days of Prayer to Overcome Darkness and Find God's Protection

When darkness presses in, how do you pray?

Scriptures & Prayers for Engaging the Enemy:

70 Days of Prayer to Rebuke the Enemy and Release God's Power

You weren't called to run from the battle—you were anointed to win it.

Scriptures & Prayers for Combating Spiritual Wickedness:

50 Days of Prayer to Overthrow Wicked Plans and Stand in God's Victory

Are you facing opposition that feels deeper than the natural? You're not imagining it—and you're not powerless.

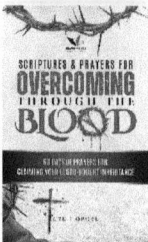

Scriptures & Prayers for Overcoming Through the Blood:

60 Days of Prayers for Claiming Your Blood-Bought Inheritance

You were never meant to fight sin, fear, or Satan in your own strength.

Standing in the Gap for Covenant Awakening:

30 Days of Prayer for National Repentance, Righteous Leadership & God's Sovereign Rule

What if your prayers could help turn the tide of a nation?

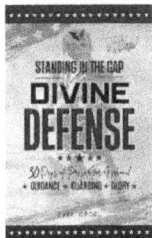

Standing in the Gap for Divine Defense:

30 Days of Prayer for National Guidance, Guarding & Glory

When the foundations of a nation feel as if they're shaking, prayer is the strongest fortress you can build.

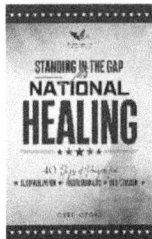

Standing in the Gap for National Healing:

40 Days of Prayer for Reconciliation, Righteousness, and Restoration

What if your prayers could help heal a nation? What if God is waiting for someone—like you—to stand in the gap?

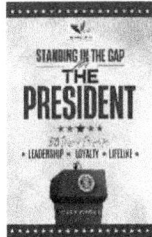

Standing in the Gap for The President:

50 Days of Prayer for Leadership, Loyalty, and Lifeline

When a nation's leader is under spiritual siege, will you answer the call to stand in the gap?

Pardon Through the Blood:

60 Days of Prayers for Total Forgiveness and Freedom

Guilt is a prison. The blood of Jesus holds the key.

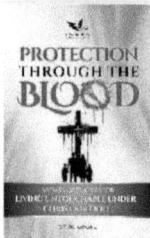

Protection Through the Blood:

60 Days of Prayers for Living Untouchable Under Christ's Blood

You are not helpless. You are not exposed. You are covered—completely—by the blood of Jesus.

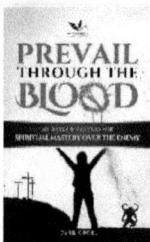

Prevail Through the Blood:

60 Days of Prayers for Spiritual Mastery Over the Enemy

What if every scheme of the enemy against your life could be dismantled—by one unstoppable weapon?

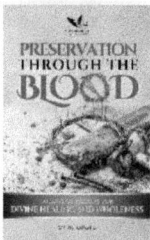

Preservation Through the Blood:

60 Days of Prayers for Divine Healing and Wholeness

Unlock Lasting Healing and Wholeness Through the Blood of Jesus

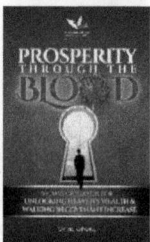

Prosperity Through the Blood:

60 Days of Prayers for Unlocking Heaven's Wealth and Walking in Covenant Increase

You were redeemed for more than survival—you were redeemed to prosper.

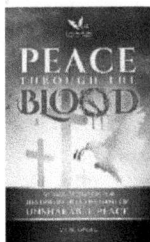

Peace Through the Blood:

60 Days of Prayers for Resting in the Covenant of Unshakable Peace

Are you ready to silence every storm of the mind, heart, and home—once and for all?